CW01509459

Words

of

Wisdom

Volume 1

© *2024 The Infinite Power of You Inc.*

amanda@theinfinitepowerofyou.com

or visit

https://amanda-rose.mykajabi.com

Cover by Daniel McCutcheon

For Cover Art Inquiries Contact mccutcheondan@gmail.com

1ˢᵗ Edition

Introduction

Life is a journey filled with moments of joy, challenges, and growth. Along the way, we encounter experiences that shape us, people who inspire us, and lessons that guide us.

Words of Wisdom is a collection born out of such moments, brought together by the unique voices of multiple authors who have traversed varied paths but share a common passion for storytelling and the profound wisdom it can impart.

This book is a tapestry of stories, insights, and life lessons that span diverse experiences and perspectives. Each section is a window into a different facet of life, offering reflections that are both personal and universal. From tales of perseverance in the face of adversity to the simple joys of everyday life, the narratives within these pages are meant to resonate with readers from all walks of life.

The power of *Words of Wisdom* lies in its ability to connect hearts and minds, to offer solace in times of difficulty, and to celebrate the beauty of human resilience and kindness.

Our aim is to provide not just stories, but insights and guidance into your own journey, illuminating your path with newfound clarity.

As you turn the pages of this book, we invite you to pause and reflect, to find yourself in the words that have been shared, and to carry forward the insights gleaned into your own life. Whether you read it cover to cover or savor each section individually, may *Words of Wisdom* serve as a trusted guide and a source of inspiration.

Thank you for embarking on this journey with us. We hope our stories and insights touch your heart and mind, leaving you enriched and inspired.

Amanda Rose & Sophie Bifield

Sherry Lee

Words of Wisdom from my Older self to my Younger Self

Dear Younger Self,

As I reflect on the journey that has brought me to where I am today, I can't help but think about the lessons I wish I had known when I was in your shoes. Life is a magnificent teacher, but sometimes, having a little guidance is helpful. So, here are ten tenets of wisdom I would share with you:

1. **Embrace Change:**

Change can be scary, but it is also inevitable. Instead of resisting it, learn to embrace it. Change brings growth, new opportunities, and unexpected adventures. Don't be afraid to take a step out of your personal comfort zone and welcome the unknown with open arms. Trust that even amid uncertainty, you have the resilience and strength to adapt and thrive. Remember, every change, big or small, is an opportunity for growth and self-discovery.

2. **Be Kind to Yourself:**

You are your own toughest critic but remember to be kind to yourself. You are human, and you will make mistakes. Instead of dwelling on your shortcomings, treat yourself with the same compassion and the same understanding that you would offer to a friend.

Celebrate your achievements, no matter how small, and forgive yourself for your imperfections. Self-love is not selfish; it is essential for your well-being. Remember that you are worthy of love and respect, just as you are, flaws and all.

3. **Follow Your Passion:**

Listen to the whispers of your heart and follow your passion fearlessly. Pursue the things that ignite a fire within you, even if they seem impractical or unconventional. Your passion is your compass, guiding you towards a life filled with purpose and fulfillment. Don't be swayed by the expectations of others; trust yourself and have the courage to chase your dreams relentlessly. Remember that success is not measured by the world's external validation or societal norms but by the fulfillment and joy you find in pursuing what sets your soul on fire.

4. **Stay Curious:**

Never lose your sense of wonder and curiosity about the world around you. Keep asking questions, seeking knowledge, and exploring new ideas. Curiosity is the key to personal growth and intellectual stimulation. Embrace every opportunity to learn and expand your horizons, whether through travel, books, or conversations with people from different walks of life. Stay curious, and the world will always remain a fascinating place. Remember that curiosity opens doors to new experiences, broadens your perspective, and keeps your mind sharp and engaged.

5. **Cherish Relationships:**

In the hustle and bustle of life, remember to cherish the relationships that matter most. Nurture your connections with family and friends, for they are the pillars of love and support in your life. Make time for more meaningful conversations, shared experiences, and moments of laughter and joy. Relationships enrich your life in ways that material possessions never can, so invest your time and energy in cultivating strong bonds with the people who bring out the best in you. Remember that true happiness lies in the quality of your relationships, not the quantity. Appreciate the people who love you unconditionally and be present for them in both good times and bad.

6. **Embrace Vulnerability:**

Life is full of ups and downs, and it's okay to show vulnerability. Embrace your emotions, both the highs and the lows and don't be afraid to express them authentically. Vulnerability is not a sign of weakness but rather a testament to your courage and authenticity. Through vulnerability, you can truly connect with others on a deeper level and cultivate genuine relationships. So, don't hide behind a facade of strength; instead, allow yourself to be vulnerable, and you'll discover the beauty in your authenticity.

7. **Practice Gratitude:**

In the hustle and bustle of your everyday life, it is easy to overlook the blessings surrounding you. Take time each day to practice gratitude for the abundance in your life, no matter how small you think it is. Gratitude will shift your focus from what you lack to a focus of what you have, fostering a sense of contentment and fulfillment. You can cultivate a gratitude practice by keeping a journal, expressing thanks to those around you, or simply taking a moment to appreciate the beauty of the world around you. Remember, gratitude is the most important key to happiness and the antidote to negativity and discontent.

8. **Embrace Failure:**

Failure is not the opposite of success; it is a

steppingstone on the path to success. Instead of fearing failure, embrace it as an opportunity for growth and learning. Every setback, mistake, or failure is a valuable lesson that teaches you resilience, perseverance, and humility. Don't let the fear of failure hold you back from pursuing your dreams; instead, see failure as a necessary part of the journey toward success. Embrace failure, learn from the failure, and use it as fuel to propel you forward toward your goals.

9. **Prioritize Self-Care:**

Self-care is not selfish. Self-care is essential for your physical, your mental, and emotional well-being. Make your self-care a priority by carving out time for activities that nourish your body, mind, and soul. Whether it be exercise, meditation, creative pursuits or simply taking time to relax and unwind, prioritize activities that recharge and rejuvenate you. Remember that you cannot pour from an empty cup, so make self-care a non-negotiable part of your routine. By taking care of yourself, you'll be better equipped to manage life's challenges and show up as the best version of yourself.

10. **Trust the Journey:**

Life is a journey that is filled with twists and turns, highs and lows, victories, and setbacks. Trust that everything happens for a reason and that you are exactly where you are meant to be. Even in the darkest moments, have faith that your struggles have a purpose and that brighter days are ahead. Trust in the timing of your life and believe that the universe has a plan for you, even if it may not always be clear. Embrace the journey with an open heart and an open mind, knowing that every experience, whether positive or negative, is shaping you into the person you are meant to become.

Dear younger self, as you navigate the twists and turns of life's journey, remember that you are capable of more than you could ever imagine. Believe in yourself, trust in your abilities, and never lose sight of the person you aspire to be. May these words of wisdom serve as a guiding light, illuminating your path and empowering you to create a life filled with purpose, passion, and fulfillment.

With love and encouragement,

Your older self

See Sherry's Books on Amazon at:

https://rb.gy/5o49e0

Connect on Facebook with Sherry at:

https://rb.gy/ujz7sg

Renny van der Deen

The Stories We Tell (Ourselves)

It was around 2010 that my experience of myself dramatically started changing. I was running a massage therapy clinic, and I signed up to a continued professional development program that not only taught an effective, injury-free way of massaging, but also communication concepts that I considered very thought-provoking and that questioned my perception of myself, my immediate surroundings, and the wider world.

And I realized that the story of my life that I told myself and others, had to change as it was full of judgments, blame, and false information. Underneath being an optimistic, smiley person leading a functional life, I was quite unhappy...

We create stories that shape our beliefs.

I learned that the way I remember something is most likely not the way it happened; I was hanging on to memories that were half-truth, half fabrication. Many of these 'made up stories' about my past were not necessarily easy to recognize, but they very much influenced my current experiences and how I related to the world around me. I turned these stories and memories into beliefs, like 'I'm not good at anything,' 'I'm not enough.' I also formed beliefs about other people: 'He's much better at that than I am,' or beliefs about what I was convinced other people thought, such as 'Nobody likes me,' 'They will never appreciate my efforts.'

Frame of reference

Ideally, whatever happens in life is considered 'neutral,' but this is not often the case. The way we experienced (or remember) our past forms, our 'frame of reference.' New experiences are filtered through this frame of reference, and we often give a positive or negative meaning to what is happening today.

However, whatever happens, happens. How we then respond (positive, neutral, or negative) is our responsibility. Becoming response-able is a skill everyone can learn; it starts with increasing awareness of the feelings and thoughts that come up, the language that is used, and the meaning that is given.

And with that, people can change their story... the one of their past as well as the one of their future. When we allow ourselves to take full responsibility for our life's journey, we step away from our 'victim story' and we become 'wise learners,' and then we start creating our future instead of living on autopilot.

Re-framing your S.T.O.R.Y.

So, I invite you to be brave...

- Catch yourself using negative or absolute language in your statements: 'not,' 'nobody,' 'never,' 'always,' and be more specific.

- Who taught you to say things like 'I should do that' or 'I must do better'? And does it resonate?

- Ask yourself: Is the story that I tell real, true, or valid? Do I *really* believe what I just said, or thought? If not, what would I like to believe instead?

Be gentle on yourself and have courage – all change starts with awareness!

When you are ready to re-frame your

S.T.O.R.Y. and become 'The Wise Learner' in your own life, I'd be honored to guide you.

Renny van der Deen – The Wise Learner Ltd

Renny, originally from The Netherlands but living in the UK since 1999, is a personal development coach, speaker, and facilitator. She currently lives in Pembrokeshire, Wales, and can often be found hiking the beautiful coastal path with her two dogs or dipping in the sea with friends any time of year, rain, or shine.

If you like the idea of growing as 'a wise learner' and changing your S.T.O.R.Y., connect with Renny:

Website: www.thewiselearner.com

Email: info@thewiselearner.com

Facebook page:

https://web.facebook.com/rennythewiselearner

Facebook group:

https://web.facebook.com/groups/thewiselearne

rcommunity

Instagram: The Wise Learner

@youarethewiselearner

Michelle Warnica

Everything is happening for you!

I believe that the Earth is a Divine school for our Soul. That we came here with a plan and mission for this life. That every challenge, obstacle, and roadblock is here with a valuable lesson realigning you to your soul's purpose. Ultimately showing you the way home to your Divine self. In a life full of lessons, one of the hardest to learn and incorporate is that *everything* is *happening for you,* not to you!

When you truly get this and integrate it into your being, life makes more sense and becomes easier to navigate. It's a difficult lesson because when the huge stuff happens, like chronic illness, divorce, job loss, financial hardship, finding the lesson is the last thing you're thinking about. For most people, the lesson, and the wisdom it brings often comes in hindsight months or years later. I'm here to help you accelerate this process.

A stroke, cancer, your spouse leaving you, whatever the event, it's all a gift from the Universe moving you into alignment with your true authentic self and greater peace and happiness.

How do I know this? Because I've experienced it in my own life more than once. I've seen it play out in the lives of many of my friends and family as well.

In 2010 I was a healthy, successful, corporate sales representative earning six figures. I had a personal trainer, drove a Lexus, and owned a condo 2 miles from multiple beaches in Southern California. From the outside it all looked like I was living the dream. It was a comfortable life. I had a friend in every city, and I was compensated well to wine and dine clients from introduction to the close and celebration of the sale. But, inside, behind closed doors I was drinking a bottle of wine or more every night. More on the weekends. I was trying to fill an emptiness that couldn't be filled with wine, food, or money. There was a longing for something more. Something to feed my soul and to ignite my passion.

One night I was home alone, drunk, and sad, crying to God. "Please help me, I know I'm here for more than this!" I warn you, be careful what you ask for because the Universe is always listening! About three weeks later my call was answered and I had a stroke! I was in the hospital paralyzed on the left side! It was the best thing that ever happened to me! Between the hospital and rehab, I was under care for exactly a month. During which time I received gift number one, a 30-day alcohol detox.

As the journey unfolded, I received multiple gifts in the form of life lessons. The two greatest gifts included compassion for me and others and accepting what is, the gift of surrender. These gifts would continue to evolve and serve me for in years to come. It was also the beginning of my sober journey. Which would also evolve and serve me for years as well.

Then in 2023, while living in a foreign country without speaking the language or having insurance, I had another devastating health situation. I slipped on a wet floor and fractured the femur head in my left hip. This accident required immediate surgery and a lengthy recovery, beginning with 30 days in bed without putting any weight on the leg.

Again, a catastrophic situation which put me on the sideline of life for a few months. But this time I knew better. Instead of asking why or feeling sorry for myself, I got busy figuring things out and setting up the 24/7 care that I needed post-surgery, then I exhaled and surrendered!

I had the wisdom and lessons from the stroke 13 years earlier to support me. Instead of taking three weeks to surrender to what is, I was there in three days. Plus, this time, I had full awareness of what was happening versus seeing the situation through the blurred lens of a brain injury.

What I was present to on this journey was a series of daily miracles. In a city where I had only lived eight months I was surrounded by support! New friends, acquaintances and strangers all stepped in to support me in any way possible! I was in such deep gratitude for this demonstration of kindness and unconditional love that I cried every day!

About two weeks later I was talking to a friend on the phone, in tears, telling her I had never felt so loved and cared for as I did with this group of Spanish speaking strangers who were my 24/7 caregivers! It was an incredible heart opening experience!

· Since then, my life has not been the same! It changed the way I see the world! I truly know that everything that's happening is here for my highest good. Here to teach me a tremendous life lesson and or to guide me to the people, places, and information that I need to expand into my greatness.

I invite you to look back on all the "worse things that ever happened to you" with a fresh lens.

Was it really the *worst thing*?

What beautiful lesson did you learn?

What magic happened as a result?

How has your life changed for the better?

Next, I invite you to consider how you can use this life lesson to help others navigate or avoid this experience. Maybe this situation was here so that you can use it to inspire and uplift others. After all that is the purpose of this life to be of service to other humans.

I invite you to spend time journaling on the worst catastrophe that you've ever experienced using the questions above. What comes up may just be the reason why you're here and what you're here to do.

Nicole Miller

My pivotal moments

I pivoted my business after spending 10 years in the same profession successfully. It was scary, but it was something I felt I had to do to create the impact that was needed. What I have learned from my pivot are lessons I feel that every entrepreneur should know. If I could go back and tell myself one thing, it would be to give myself grace. As entrepreneurs we all struggle with this, and it was no different for me through my pivot. I wanted everything to come together just as it was, as a virtual assistant.

One of my favorite quotes is by Jon Acuff and it truly helped me through my pivot when my mindset was falling awry.

"Don't compare your beginning to someone else's

middle, or your middle to someone else's end." — **Jon Acuff**

Pivots take time and you can't compare the beginning of your pivot to the end of what you were doing previously. There will also probably be a lot of trial and error through your pivot, and you need to remain open for those moments of learning. Know that success comes in more forms than just monetary and be okay with that.

I found more success in being seen as a passionate mentor than I have financially. People are paying attention and that's where the impact comes from.

I remember feeling like I had it all wrong when pieces weren't fitting together as a mentor in the same way they did for me as a virtual assistant. It was maddening, but then I realized that things were going to be different with a pivot from one profession to another, even if the stronghold of my niche is relative.

Understand there's no fixed rule on how long a pivot can take. That transition period can be quick, or it can take time. Think about when you first started any business — it takes time. How much time is truly going to depend on many factors such as visibility and outreach results. Believe in yourself, as cliche as that sounds. Mindset will help you so much during your pivot. Commit to yourself to put in the work. Pay attention to the details.

Contact: nicole@nicolemillermediainc.com

Instagram:

https://www.instagram.com/nicolemillermediai nc/

Website: https://www.nicolemillermediainc.com

Sheri Queen

Embracing the Journey: Wisdom from a Late-Blooming Author

Imagine telling your younger self that the path to your dreams isn't a sprint, but a marathon, one that you would start earnestly only after crossing the 50-year milestone. That's precisely the journey I embarked on when I decided to chase my dream of becoming an author by enrolling in an MFA program for writing popular fiction at Seton Hill University.

At first, I was intimidated. The classroom, filled with younger peers, made me wonder if I had missed my moment. But as I dove into the learning experience, a profound realization took hold: education, especially in the arts, knows no age. It was a lesson in humility and courage, teaching me to embrace every opportunity to gain experience, irrespective of the stage in life.

Do you remember a time when you thought it was too late for you to pursue your passion? How did you overcome that barrier?

The journey from student to published author was fraught with self-doubt. When my first fiction book, *Bounty Huntress (Sleepy Hollow Hunter Book One)*, was published, imposter syndrome whispered incessantly. The key to silencing those doubts was focusing on one step at a time, acknowledging each small achievement on the path to greater confidence.

Can you recall a moment when you doubted your abilities? What small step helped you move forward?

One of the most significant challenges I faced was balancing my role as a caregiver with my academic and writing endeavors. Caring for a newborn while earning my MFA taught me that sometimes life demands we slow down so we can absorb the lessons along the way. Supporting my now eleven-year-old grandchild's emotional and sensory challenges reminds me that our personal experiences and the support we provide to others enrich our storytelling and make it more relatable.

Have you ever had to juggle personal responsibilities with pursuing your goals? How did it shape your journey?

To anyone with the desire to fulfill a secret dream, remember: it's okay to move at your own pace. The journey isn't a race against others but a series of steps towards self-fulfillment. Here are a few takeaways that guided me and might help you:

1. **Embrace Learning at Any Age**: Whether you're 25, 50, or older, it's never too late to pursue

your passion. Every class, book, and experience are a steppingstone towards your goal.

2. **Overcome Imposter Syndrome with Small Wins**: Celebrate every success, minor or major. Each one is proof of your capabilities and a step towards building confidence.

3. **Balance Is Key:** Do the best you can to balance your goals and responsibilities. It won't always be even but keep trying.

4. **Pace Yourself:** Your journey is yours alone. Rushing might lead to burnout. Don't lose the joy along the way.

Ask yourself: What step can I take today that will bring me closer to my dream? The rest of your life begins now, and it's never too late to pursue what truly matters to you.

Sheri Queen writes immersive stories of adventure and romance, with a heavy dose of magic, set in the modern world.

Join her on her latest fictional journey at www.sheriqueen.com.

You can find her socializing with her readers here:

Facebook:
https://www.facebook.com/SheriQueenAuthor

Instagram:
https://www.instagram.com/authorsheriqueen/

Khwan Hathai

The Money Epiphany: Never Just Numbers, Always Emotions

Throughout my years advising high-net-worth individuals and families in wealth management, I uncovered a poignant truth: real prosperity doesn't reside in the sheer abundance of wealth; it blossoms through our emotional connections with money. Inspired by this epiphany, I founded Epiphany Financial Therapy, a place committed to helping individuals achieve both financial and emotional well-being.

The traditional symbols of success—luxurious cars, sprawling estates, and extravagant travels—often portray a misleading image of wealth. When we take a moment to look deeper, we discover that true wealth is not about the figures in our bank account, but about how well our wealth resonates with our heart's deepest desires. It's about crafting a life where our resources do more than just sustain; they enrich our passions and empower our aspirations.

Imagine saving for a home as not merely an investment but as crafting a nest of warmth, love, and security—a space where every corner resonates with cherished memories. Or think of investing in education not just for the potential financial returns but as a commitment to ignite dreams, fueling personal growth and lifelong learning.

This fresh perspective transformed my approach to personal finance. I began to set goals that pulse with emotional energy and purpose. These aren't just financial targets; they are dreams that guide us, serving as beacons that illuminate our path through life's challenges and resonate deeply with our souls calling.

Embracing this holistic and dynamic perspective, I invite you to view your finances not just as numbers, but as a vibrant reflection of your deepest dreams and values. This approach transforms financial planning into an act of weaving your aspirations into the fabric of your daily life, each decision driven by a powerful "why." Rooted in love and commitment, this "why" turns financial planning from a routine task into an enthusiastic and fulfilling journey. Understand that the true emotional weight of money can deeply influence your financial plans, turning money management into a meaningful dialogue about your goals and desires.

With the launch of Epiphany Financial Therapy, my goal transcended merely filling a market gap—I aimed to forge a path toward holistic financial wellness that integrates cognitive, emotional, behavioral, and relational health. This initiative is not just a method; it's a movement dedicated to transforming the financial landscape into one where every decision, from investments to savings, profoundly enriches our life, making our financial journey as emotionally rewarding as it is materially successful.

As you embrace this money epiphany, understand that your financial vitality is not measured by the wealth you accumulate, but by how deeply your financial choices resonate with your core values and aspirations. Let this realization do more than just enhance your financial status—it should enrich your whole being, bringing not only material wealth but also a profound sense of peace, balance, and happiness. Here's to a journey that transcends mere numbers, fully embracing your emotions and transforming every aspect of your life with each thoughtful step you take.

Get in touch:

Website:

https://www.epiphanyfinancialtherapy.com

Linkedin:

https://www.linkedin.com/in/khwanhathai

Instagram:

https://www.instagram.com/khwanepiphany

Facebook page:

https://www.facebook.com/EpiphanyFT

Email: Khwan@epiphanyfinancialtherapy.com

Rebecca Nicoll

Live the life you love

Words of Wisdom. I admit I laughed when I thought about being considered Wise. But then I realized that Words of Wisdom are around more often than you think. In books, movie quotes, even something someone says in passing can strike something deeply within you that counts as Wisdom.

Here are some Words of Wisdom that have resonated with me, and now I bequeath to you:

1. Do It True.

If you haven't seen the Banger Sisters with Goldie Hawn and Susan Sarandon, you should! However, the eldest daughter gives a Valedictorian Speech. It really smacked me when she said she'd "rather fail doing what *she* wants to do, than to succeed and live life miserable by living someone else's dreams." Do it for *you* and do it *true*.

I spent quite some time trying to be what I thought I *should* be and not doing what I genuinely loved. Every day was difficult. No matter how happy I thought I was making everyone else, my own soul was not feeling it. In the end I had a melt down and ranted about how I was doing everything they wanted and life sucked, only to find out they didn't have those expectations in the first place – huh? Years of wasting my life trying to live up to non-existent expectations!

This was a *huge* breakthrough for me as I then had to think about what I really wanted in life. My life. No one else. Whose life are we here to live if not our own?

2. Not all those who wander are lost.

This famous Tolkien quote can be taken a few diverse ways. As a flight attendant I travel for a living, so this quote is appropriate in more than one way for me, however, today it's about the meandering path of life. Not everyone is taking the same route. They may not even have the same destination and goals as you do – so why are you comparing your road to theirs?

I wandered for *years* before I figured out even the direction, I wanted to be going but that does not make my wandering any less valid than yours. Despite not becoming a flight attendant until I was thirty, I was not lost. My road just took me on a route that allowed me to learn what I needed to get to where I am today.

3. If you've got the chance take it, take it while you've got the chance.

Absolute best as song by Cody Johnson called 'Til you can't. It reminds us that our time is limited; so, get out there and live life whilst we have it.

We can make plans for the future and talk about what we'll do when we retire or how things will be in ten years but today is the only thing, we are sure to have. The same opportunity given to you today might not be here tomorrow, and neither might you be.

I am a slow learner, so it took me until my mid-thirties to find my passion in having my own little business that helps others. This came at a time when I was searching, and my friend opened the opportunity. This business is steadily changing my life, those of my customers and, team. Imagine if I hadn't taken that chance?

4. Feel the Fear – and do it anyway!

This is the title of a personal development book I came across a few years ago by Susan Jeffers. So many people look at entrepreneurs and businesspeople and think I could never do that. Multiple excuses may come up. But really, it's the overwhelm and the fear taking control.

Do you think said entrepreneurs and businesspeople don't feel fear? We do! It is not about being fearless. It's about what you do with that fear that creates your future.

Do you let it control you and make you sit back in the comfort zone? Do you listen to all those naysayers (whom might even be family or close friends)? Or do you push through the fear, use it, and do the scary thing anyway? Do you take the risk and leave your comfort zone?

I chose to Feel the Fear and Do It Anyway and

my life has gone onwards and upwards. Never allow it to be fears choice. Make it yours.

5. It's a big ball of wibbly, wobbly, timy, wimy ... stuff.

This quite famous Doctor Who quote by David Tennant made me think a bit more about how I perceive time.

There are two sides to this: there's only so much of it in life so get off your ass and Live! Do the amazing thing you've been putting off because what if you aren't here tomorrow?

I have a bucket list that's a mile long. However, only recently have I been doing what's on it. I kept thinking "One day." But, what if one day doesn't come? Can you look back on your life and think — yep that was worth it? This concept gave me that push to fly, to travel, and to start my business, to help others live their dreams to. Don't wait until tomorrow. Live your life now.

The other side of time is that people think time has already passed them by. What they don't realize is that it's never too late till you're dead. Alan Rickman didn't become an actor till later in life. JK Rowling was thirty-two when the first Harry Potter Book came out. The Colonel was sixty-two when he started KFC. The man who invented cup noodles invented the Space Ramen when he was ninety-five! If they can do it, why not me? Why not you? Whether it be losing weight, going on that holiday, opening a business, whatever it's for, you decide and *do it.*

6. Find your why.

Not actually quoting anyone that I'm aware of for this one but it's an important thing for me. I spent *years* trying to lose weight. I've always been the big girl, especially throughout my school career where I was bullied about this. But trying to lose weight to fit into an idea of what others thought I should look like wasn't something that motivated me. I'd do it for a time but then I'd take a rest day, then a rest week, then I wasn't doing anything.

Fear I find is not a particularly good motivator in this aspect. It wasn't until I sat down and looked at *why* I wanted to lose weight and focused on the positives instead. I wanted to be healthier so that I could travel more. I wanted to go bungee jumping and not stress about being the "maximum weight." I wanted to fit on the rides at theme parks. I wanted to have less weight to carry on my joints while I was exploring other cultures. It was no longer about running from bullying or doing what others wanted but, about doing what I loved.

Now that I've lost over 20kg I have a business that helps others to follow their own health goals. I'd call that a fantastic why.

Figure out your why and no one can stop you!

People can follow me on Facebook at:

https://web.facebook.com/BigBouncingFlea

Or join my Facebook group at:

https://web.facebook.com/groups/11744209663 58139

Norma Brščič

From: younger me

To: me

Subject: I want your help

Hey there!

So, I read your contribution to the
Word of Wisdom collection and
decided to reach out. Thank you for
spreading hope to us who are still
in the trenches of trauma recovery
and getting our relationships out
of the constant mess.

I loved how well you worded what happened to you. Everything about how you *used* to identify as a sex abuse victim/survivor and now it's not a part of your identity anymore but just one of the things that happened in your life.

How you wanted nothing but to create a happy and stable environment for your children and a loving marriage for yourself but felt so hopeless. Like you, I didn't see any successful marriage model anywhere either. I seriously doubt I will be able to break that pattern alone. I struggle to find a healthy relationship; all my past connections have been problematic.

What touched me the most was when you described that you found a way not only to learn to live with all that happened to you but, also to release the pain of your memories, the flashbacks, and the triggers that brought all the disgust, fear, and panic back to the surface. I've never heard that's possible, and I've been in therapy for years and I have tried other approaches.

Also, your explanation about how the abandonment wound is the core wound of anyone who experienced trauma had hit home for me. Your insight that every trauma involves feelings of abandonment — whether it be through abuse or neglect by those who should have cared for us; resonated deeply. You worded so many things that were inside me and for the first time I felt noticed and personally addressed.

Describing your journey to recovery was a huge revelation for me. How everyone was telling you that you cannot really heal from sexual abuse and that you can only learn to live with it. Your strength when you didn't take that for your truth and kept going until you got the results you wanted!

The section where you discussed trauma being stored in the body and your method for releasing it has left me intrigued and I can't stop thinking about it.

Is it really possible to get better? To stop feeling abandoned? To feel like you truly belong, and to not just pretend. To find someone who will love me for me. I feel worthless. I am so tired of this. My boyfriend recently broke up with me. That was my healthiest relationship so far. It ended. I feel this giant void and I just can't do it anymore.

There is nothing I want more than my story to end how yours ended, by breaking the cycle of toxic relationships, finding the right partner, breaking the generational trauma, and creating a stable, loving marriage which is a healthy base for your offspring.

Now tell me, how do I become you?

Connect with Norma

Facebook

profile: https://www.facebook.com/norma.brscic

Facebook

group: https://web.facebook.com/groups/11489
01526057706

Email: norma.svn@gmail.com

Veronica Salazar

Stay You

Success looks different for everyone. Some of us get stuck in thinking that there is only one way to *be* successful. I always felt that you must look and act a certain part. Be someone and something different than who you really were. I would mimic those around me that I considered successful.

I did this for years and I found myself angry and sad majority of the time. My weight would fluctuate up and down. Stressed because I felt like was constantly being judged. I was afraid that if I were truly me, people would not like me or do business with me. I was always told to act this way not that. Or wear this, not that. So, I thought that if I was the real me it was wrong.

This was just one of the many times I got lost in

my journey. It's easy to do.

Don't try to fit in

In the beginning stages of my business, I found myself changing to "fit in." I wanted to be around those that I considered "successful." Somehow, I held them to a high standard in my mind. I felt like they were at a level much higher than me. I did not feel I was worthy the way I was to be a "successful" business owner. Or that I could even measure up. It took me years to figure out that I was just like them. A person. An entrepreneur. A business owner.

I was afraid to be the real me. What if they do not like me? What if I offend them by being me? I was afraid to display my weirdness and quirkiness. Yet I was so angry all the time and could not see why. I just get teary-eyed thinking about all the time spent living like this. Years of unhappiness. When you have been told things over and over, it takes a while to break that belief and create a new one. Listen to who you are. Believe in who you are. Follow the beat of your own drum.

Guess what happened when I finally decided to show up as me? I did not feel angry anymore. I felt like I could breathe again. The goals and bucket list items that I had put on paper each year, going unaccomplished, were now being done. I found people smiling back at me because I was smiling. I would NOT be where I am today if I had kept trying to fit in or listened to what others told me how I had to be. My suggestion to you is that from time to time, ask yourself questions.

Questions such as: Are you being your true self? What are you afraid to say? What are you afraid to do? Are you wearing what *you* like? Is that the haircut you really want? Have you wanted to dye your hair a vibrant color, but you have been afraid to? Do you want to start a business? Are you afraid that you will be ridiculed or rejected? Are you compromising what you want so that you can please someone else?

I went through so many moments of living the life that other people wanted for me. And when I would choose another way or path, they would act like I was incapable of making the right decision. Sometimes people *think* they know what is best for you, but really you are the only one that truly knows.

What do you want to do? Where do you want to go? Do you know what your core values are? Have you thought about that? I learned that your core values guide you in creating the life that you want. When I figured out what my core values were, I could pinpoint specific moments in my life where I was living true to those values. I was happy. I felt free.

Most of the time these people who offer their advice or voice their opinion about what you are doing are not taking action themselves. Take a good look. Are they going after their goals? Are they doing the same thing you are? Have they done what you are trying to do? I can almost guarantee that they are not or have not. Even though it is hard to not hear what they are saying, because let's face it is hard to not hear them, don't fucking *listen* to them!

Dreams do come true.

It is possible for dreams to come true. Anyone who tells you different is wrong. What are your dreams? Have you thought about it? Have you said it aloud? There is something about hearing yourself say what your dreams are. The universe works in mysterious ways to make our dreams come true. But you must tell it what you want. How it comes true is not for you to worry about. All you must do is believe it is yours. I know this to be a fact. Do not discount the power of the universe.

My spouse and I would stare at the house across the street. It was a cute, white wood-framed home with a big picture window in the living room. We would daydream about what it would be like sipping coffee, watching the snow fall from that window. After years of staring, I got the idea of leaving a note on the door asking if they were ever interested in selling the house to let us know. We weren't really looking to buy, but I was putting it out in the universe. Six months had passed, and nothing came of the note left on their door. So, one day I told my spouse that we should start looking at houses. since we keep dreaming about the one across the street. We did not know if we qualified to buy a house. I had not even talked to a lender. We did not have money for a down payment. I was just thinking what if?

After seeing two houses the following weekend, guess who showed up at our door? Yes. The people from across the street. They asked if we were still interested in the house. I could not believe it. Was this really happening? I was speechless. They gave us a tour of the house and it was everything we had imagined it to be. But what about financing? The down payment? As I mentioned before, we had not even thought that far. Then it felt like the universe was putting all the energy forces in our favor because within a week we had the cash to buy the house. And thirty days later we were moving in. I still get goosebumps thinking about how it all happened. We stared at that house for four years and one day decided to leave a note.

So, when people say that dreams do not come true. They're wrong. Dreams *do* come true. What are your dreams?

Reflection:

I remember this time years ago, early in my business, I lived an hour and fifteen minutes away from my clients. I drove into town twice a week for appointments. Well one day I had to cancel my appointments because I did not have enough money for gas to get to town. Has that ever happened to you? Not having money for gas? Of course, I made up an excuse. I was not going to really tell them why I could not make it. I felt so small that day. So unsuccessful. These moments are so important to remember. The trials and tribulations we go through. These reflections can help push you forward during the tough times.

Reflecting on your journey can also help make you realize how strong you are. A map showing you that you have survived some of the toughest storms. So, if you are trying to reach a goal and you question if you are capable, do a little reflection.

Final note:

Everyone else's opinion can get in the way. I allowed myself to believe those others' opinions. I believed them for a long time. It made me question who I was and why the real me was not good enough to be. Do not let that happen to you. Figure out who you are. Do not try to fit in. Find out what your core values are so you have a guide. Do a little reflection. Believe that dreams do come true. And most importantly stay you.

Veronica Salazar

Email: veronica@billabillzllc.com

Website: www.billabillzllc.com

Facebook:

https://web.facebook.com/BillaBillzLLC

Instagram:

https://www.instagram.com/billabillzllc/

Malissa Collins

Forgiveness gave me freedom.

I want to tell you a story of a scared little girl named Missy. She had to grow up faster than any child should. See Missy was sexually abused by her biological father. She learned things that no child from an early age shouldn't have to know. As she got older, she used to read as a way out of the real world. Into a world where children could be kids and live a happy life. Not a life of always having to watch your back because you never know when he's coming.

I'm going to tell you a quick story of this event that took place. It was about 6 am after my mother left for work. On that morning mom was telling dad she had to leave soon, or she would be later for work. At that moment my heart sank, I knew what was about to happen. So, I got up quietly and locked my bedroom door and got back into bed in the fetal position with my back against the wall praying he wasn't coming into my room. I could hear mom headed toward the kitchen and out the door and my father saying good-bye. I threw the covers over my head and suddenly I could hear the wrestle of the doorknob. My Father unlocks the door, open it, picks me up, and takes me to his room and has sex with me.

This continued until I was 14 years old, and I decided it was time to put an end to it. I fought him off. He got mad and put a gun to my head and threatened me. The next day I went to school and tried to take my own life in the bathroom. Thanks to a friend walking in she saved my life.

Fast forward to my adult life I had to find a way to overcome this childhood trauma, so I figured out a technique that worked for me. I wrote a long letter to my father telling him everything under the sunshine and at the end of that letter I said I forgive you, I am no one to judge you here on earth. When you're standing in front on your judgement day you will be judged. For now, your punishment will be here on earth.

At that moment I felt as if a mountain had lifted off me and the shackles opened. I was finally free from all that torment I endured. There is nothing like freedom. You must find a way to heal and live your best life.

While you are depressed, your perpetrator is living their best lives. He is not thinking about you. When they realize that they no longer have control over you. They start to fade in the background. I have helped so many young girls and women telling my story and how I overcame sexually abuse and I am still stand with my head high and living what is my best life right now.

Email: AuthorMalissaCollins@gmail.com

Phone: 321-961-4128

Mercedes Aspland

Be bold!

It's so easy to get caught up in the little things, isn't it? We spend so much time worrying about what others think about us and our decisions. By doing that, we're putting our dreams on hold. And we're forgetting something crucial – our own happiness. It's like we're stuck in a loop, trying to meet expectations that aren't even our own.

I've found a personal mantra helpful during these times: "*You never regret the things you do, only the things you don't do.*" This phrase is not only about being brave; it's about empowering ourselves to step out of our comfort zones. I use it to remind myself to choose action over inaction. It's led me to live a life filled with a wide range of experiences. Sure, not every project or adventure has been perfect. But each one has taught me something valuable. And that's the beauty of it – learning and growing from each step we take.

So, I want to share this with you: **Be bold**. Make the choices that excite you, that challenge you. The things that make your life unique. It's not about pleasing everyone; it is about finding what resonates with you. Remember, you are not alone in this. We are all working through life's ups and downs. Sometimes, what we need most is a reminder that it's okay to focus on our well-being and desires.

Think about this – what's one thing you've always wanted to do but held back, because of others' opinions? Now imagine taking that step, not with recklessness, but with a sense of purpose and joy. Imagine the stories you'll tell and the memories you'll create. These are the moments that shape us, that add color and depth to our lives.

Here is something else to consider. Being true to ourselves isn't self-centered; it's about being authentic. It's about doing things that align with our inner selves, not our external circumstances. When we do this, we not only enrich our lives but also inspire those around us to do the same. We become a positive force, encouraging others to follow their paths and dreams.

So, take that step. Grasp the life you have always imagined, not only for yourself, but as an example for others. It's about creating a life that feels right for you and, in turn, spreads positivity to those around you. Let's all aim for a life where we don't leave room for 'what ifs'. Instead, we fill it with 'what is' – a life full of passion, authenticity, and joy.

Facebook group:

https://www.facebook.com/groups/spiritualemp oweredwomen

https://www.itacommunity.com/conscious-creators-community

Email: mercedes@itacommunity.com

Evelina Åström

The Elevator Journey That Would Turn Out to Be a Nightmare (And A Wake-Up Call)

I entered the elevator when I saw my supervisor approaching. The presence of my supervisor always made me feel insecure, as her hostility persisted since I gained my position. So, I held the elevator for her in an attempt to make peace with her, and she walked in.

The journey up would turn out to be a nightmare. Her eyes narrowed with anger as she accused me of not doing my job and being a disappointment. Nothing that she said was true, but her voice got louder and louder. The elevator stopped, and she continued claiming I didn't do my job out in the corridor, making it possible for colleagues and patients to hear what she accused me of.

I was so tired of having to set boundaries all the time and being the victim of other people's anger when I had done nothing to justify her action. I wanted a peaceful life without confrontations.

Ever wondered why having challenging conversations makes you feel deflated afterwards?

I know you can stand up for yourself if you must. You have practiced setting healthy boundaries for a long time now, but after each confrontation addressing someone's behavior, you still find yourself enveloped in sadness. You ask yourself why confrontations always diminish your life force. I have the answer to your question and the solution.

The thing is you live in a world shaped by non-sensitive leaders. You have learned how to ignore your gut feelings. You have learned to feel ashamed of your emotions. You have learned that the only way to survive in this society is to stop being sensitive.

So, let me ask you this: Who has taught you how to manage people that confront you? The answer, my friend, is often a non-sensitive person.

The reason why you always feel so down when confronted, no matter how good you are at standing up for yourself, is because you manage confrontations like a non-sensitive person, and that's not an approach that feels aligned for most

highly sensitive people (and to be frank, it attracts confrontations). Instead, you need to act aligned with your heart, decode your emotions and

embrace them as your compass.

Your emotions are the passage to where

the realms of wisdom lie.

It's the emotions that help you detect darkness in the world. It's your emotions that help you face the truth that everyone else is avoiding. It is your emotions that tell you if a person is acting with ego or not.

Being highly sensitive means we have a sensitive, open heart, and we feel deeply. But what we feel is the truth that others are denying. When someone confronts you, they stop you from accessing this inner wisdom of yours that I call the 'Feminine Light.' Your sensitive and kind heart is the gateway to the wisdom this world needs, and it is time you guard your 'Feminine Light' when confronted.

By Evelina Åström, A Swedish Trauma-Informed Leadership Mentor & Relationship Expert

Specialized in Confrontation Management for Highly Sensitive Big-Hearted Female Entrepreneurs.

Contact Information:

Facebook:

https://www.facebook.com/evelinaastrom.co/

LinkedIn:

https://www.linkedin.com/in/evelinaåström/

Instagram:

https://www.instagram.com/evelinaastrom.co/

Website: https://evelinaastrom.com

Email: info@evelinaastrom.com

Get Evelina's FREE Gift 'How To Escape People With Hidden Agendas On Social Media':

https://evelinaastrom.myflodesk.com/escape

Melissa Marie Watson

And So Are You

Epiphanies: Powerful, intuitive insights that pop into a mind.

Enlightenment: the soul-level-epiphany. Personally, I am an old soul. My soul has been through it. How do I know? Because old souls come to Earth with a purpose, a mission, and it usually includes overcoming tough shit.

The biggest thing I've had to overcome was my lack of self-love. I've used a whole slew of less-than-honorable coping methods: serial dating, sex, sugar, carbs, shopping, alcohol, partying, accomplishments, titles. Distractions. I was overpowered by *fear*. I desperately wanted to be okay, so I hid deeper and deeper within myself in a whole different space than where I hid the things that I couldn't face.

However, distractions only cover up the problem as it continues to brew. I had to face it. What I found was that I still didn't love myself fully. I'd get into a relationship and my focus would go there. Suddenly, my worth was tied to it. It became easy to lose myself in other people. Like I was afraid to be okay within myself. It was as if I feared I would eventually tire and fall apart. Like I'd suffocate or drown in my own mess. I hate to say it, but I was unknowingly waiting for someone to show up and save me. I've held on for this long, but how much longer can I last? Self-doubt still lingered deep within.

I've felt love for myself, but I unintentionally decided it had to be conditional. My self-love has evolved over the years - this is why they call healing a journey. Healing keeps going until death. And beyond. But I believe the point of death happens when we've fulfilled our intended level of healing and growth at a soul level.

At my point of enlightenment, self-love became visceral. Unconditional. Otherworldly. It shook me to my core and showered me in warm light. It far exceeded falling in love with another human. It bubbled over and brought me to tears. It gave me the sense of floating, as I shed my skin, I became weightless. I've known for a long time that I am a spiritual being but knowing it and being it at a soul-level are two different things. I awakened the pure and unconditional love of God that is within all of us.

If I had to pinpoint one thing that brought it on, it was simply becoming the observer - being aware of everything but knowing it couldn't touch me. Letting events, thoughts, and emotions be felt and seen, then letting them dissipate before they could stick. Become untouchable but open your heart to let the light pour in.

Where I came from and where I am going is connected to everything. Enlightenment for me is surrender. It is being everything at a soul level. It means being okay with the things that cause pain and fear because regardless of anything I have done, I remain untouched. Who I am is The Universe, love, light, a sliver of God. And so are you.

Melissa Marie Watson, M.Ed., owner, and founder of Envisioned Life Institute LLC

Website: www.envisionedlifeinstitute.com

Instagram: https://www.instagram.com/envisionedlifeinstitute/

Facebook:

https://web.facebook.com/MelissaMarieWatson1

TikTok:

https://www.tiktok.com/@melissamariewatson1

Lynsey Scott

"Cherish the moments spent together, for it is in these moments that the true magic unfolds."

As I reflect on the journey home-educating my children, a choice that has been the most rewarding decision I've ever made, I can see the parallels between this choice and my decision to build my own spiritual and life coaching business now the children are older. I wanted my children to have a childhood that nurtured their strengths and challenges. But most of all, I could not get my head around putting my young child's care into the hands of strangers. The idea of skipping school resonated with me on a deep level. Home education offered the flexibility and freedom I believed would best serve my family.

And so, with a heart full of determination, I embarked on this journey.

My eldest, Harmony, was born with a medical condition requiring many surgeries and a disability that I knew would initially make her reliant on others who could not have her best interests at heart the way I could. I researched the best ways to support her, and I made effort to get to know and liaise with adults who shared her disability and were living independent lives.

Unlike the rigid structure of traditional schooling, home education empowered me to tailor my approach to suit each child's learning style and pace. School is not the only option. As parents, we have the autonomy to provide a child-led experience and ignite a love for learning.

Through this experience, I've kept the following questions in mind: What kind of learners are my children? What passions drive them? How can I support and nurture their individuality?

Our path has not been simply sitting around the table with workbooks. They say it takes a village to raise a child, and although this 'village' was not visible at first, I made it my mission to provide my children with a team of role models, mentors, and friends. I opened our house to invite other families to play and learn with us and hired experts in their fields to come and share their passions with the children.

When my health took a downward spiral, I was able to adapt and delegate tasks which I could no longer carry out myself.

If I could go back in time and offer advice to my younger self, I would say this: Trust your instincts and have faith in your children and yourself. Embrace the messiness of family life and see every challenge as an opportunity for growth.

And above all, cherish the moments spent together, for it is in these moments that the true magic unfolds.

Home education is not just a method of schooling—it's a way of life. It is about nurturing a love for learning and empowering children to become lifelong learners. Somewhere along our parenting journey, we realize this is also true for our adult selves. I am filled with gratitude for the wisdom gained and the countless blessings that home-educating my children has brought me. Might you consider it too?

Lynsey Scott

Email: ThoughtfulGuidance@consultant.com

https://linktr.ee/thoughtfultarotguidance

Website: www.thoughtfultarotguidance.com

Andreia Ferreira

Keep being you

Becoming an entrepreneur is a life-changing journey. Showing up for your business is another transformative journey, mostly if you are a shy and introverted fempreneur who suffers from deep anxiety about going on camera like I was. If you can relate to this, congratulations! You are not alone, and you're meant to read this.

Let's dive into some wisdom that will spark your heart especially if you want to align your personal brand with your essence. Authenticity has become such a buzzword! "Authenticity is your secret sauce!" Seriously, it is! It's what sets you apart in a sea of sameness. Before you search for it outside. Please, do it right! Your authenticity is in yourself, in your essence! Have the courage to show the real you – quirks, flaws, and all. Your audience will appreciate the genuine connection, trust me.

Now, let's talk about confidence. Waiting to be confident to take the first step will make you not take action at all! Confidence is like a muscle; you need to make the workout for it to grow. If you keep seated on the couch waiting for it to grow... it won't! Start small and keep up, the more mistakes you make the more you learn, and before you know it, you'll be comfortable in front of the camera. Your personal image? It's like your calling card. Make sure it speaks YOU fast and clear. Notice I said, "speaks YOU"?

Ditch the cookie-cutter "look professional" corporate approach if that doesn't relate to you and the message you want to send. Inject your personality into every detail. You're not for everyone, and not all high-paying clients wear a suit, in short - there is space for your uniqueness!

Is privacy important to you, and you don't want to share all your life out there? Good news! You don't have to! You decide which part of your journey and life (struggles and wins included) you will share. You can share only 10% but make them 100% true! Share your story and remember that your business is not about you, it's about your ideal people. Be intentional and share what will resonate and benefit them. Someone out there needs to hear exactly what you have to say.

Finally, consistency! Yes, I said it! Before you roll up your eyes, keep with me. It's your business, you get to decide what consistency means to you. Also, remember that consistency is not just about how many times you show up, but also how you show up.

Do you keep up with your branding,

message, posture, beliefs, and values? Yes, we are always evolving, and we are allowed to change, but if you do it at any given minute your ideal people will get confused, won't build trust with you, and will go away.

Most importantly, keep being *you.*

So, there you have it - some heartfelt nuggets of wisdom to sprinkle into your mind and heart. You've got this! I'm cheering for you! *Bloom!*

ANDREIA FERREIRA

Personal Brand Image Mentor & Consultant

Show Up - Introvert Fempreneur Community:

Facebook group:
https://www.facebook.com/groups/showupwith andreiacommunity

Instagram:
https://www.instagram.com/showupwithandreia

YouTube:

https://www.youtube.com/@showupwithandreia

Email: andreiapersonalbrand@gmail.com

Gabriella Guarnerio

From Graphic Designer to Faceless Digital Marketer

As a 43-year-old mom raising an autistic child, I never imagined I'd find my calling in the world of faceless digital marketing. But when traditional jobs failed to provide the flexibility and income I desired, I took a leap of faith. I invested half of my savings into building an online business I could run remotely, on my own terms. And let me tell you - it was the best decision I ever made.

The beauty of faceless digital marketing is that it truly levels the playing field. You don't need a fancy studio, camera crew, or even to show your face to the world. All you need is a smartphone, an internet connection, and the courage to invest in yourself.

I started by creating a simple digital product

through Canva, packaging up my hard-earned wisdom on a topic I was passionate about. From there, I launched a faceless Instagram account and committed to consistently sharing value-driven content - 3 reels per day and ten story posts to stay top-of-mind with my audience.

Those early days of constant content creation while juggling mom life were tough, but pushing through that grind phase was critical. Showing up relentlessly for your audience is how you earn their trust and position yourself as the solution to their needs. Before I knew it, sales started rolling in from my digital offer.

But this isn't only about making money - it's about changing lives through the transformation you provide.

I don't simply sell products; I sell outcomes and the vision of who someone can become by applying my teachings. If this work-at-home mom could manifest a wildly successful online business from scratch, so can you. The world of faceless digital marketing is a great equalizer where your mindset, not your circumstances, determines your income potential.

I'm living proof that you can build an empire from your smartphone. All you need is the courage to invest in your dreams as I did. Take that first step. Unlock the freedom and fulfillment of faceless digital entrepreneurship. Your future self will thank you.

Connect with me on Instagram or visit my website for more insights on mastering the faceless digital marketing game. If you can dream it, you can do it.

Instagram:

https://www.instagram.com/fiercefemininequotes/

Website:

https://facelessbusinessblog.systeme.io/ubc

Wendy Raven Johnson

Be unapologetically you!

Dear Younger, Me,

As you stand at the crossroad in the quiet, snow-blanketed streets of our small town in Ontario, Canada, I'm reaching out from the future to provide you wisdom of our journey ahead. The path from where I am now, on the sun-drenched shores of Florida, is one rich with challenges and transformation.

Let me first say that I see you, I hear you, I am proud of you, and I love you. This letter isn't just a reflection on life but rather to share my experiences to steer you away from the darkness of conformity and into the light of authenticity. Leaving everything familiar behind and moving to Florida was terrifying, yet it was the start of our transformation to being our authentic, unapologetic self.

Right now, you are conforming to the expected norms - saying the right things, wearing the right clothes, and living a life scripted by "shoulds" and expectations that rule your life and smother your true desires.

You often play the roles written by others - roles that never quite fit, no matter how hard you try to conform. You are the queen of nodding yes, when let's be honest, you want to shout hell no at the top of your lungs. Trying to live your life people-pleasing and for others approval is like trying to quench thirst with salty water. Spoiler alert: it doesn't work!

Change, while terrifying, is also the gateway to discovering who we truly are. I learned that change is the only reliable constant and embracing it is not just an option, but a necessity for growth.

Girl, let me tell you we have huge changes in our life that come from the most challenging days. You will face trials that seem insurmountable - single motherhood, raising two kids, toxic relationships, being homeless and the loss of our parents - these will test you like nothing else. But believe me, these heartaches are not just obstacles; they are opportunities to find your strength.

These moments teach you the true meaning of resilience. It's not about bouncing back to the old you - heck no, it's about using tough times to choose a new path that is a whole lot truer to who you are!

Understanding that authenticity is the foundation of a fulfilled life was the turning point for our life. Embracing your true self takes having a strong inner connection to your ideals and expressing them fearlessly and unapologetically. Living authentically means tearing down the facade of perfection and letting go of the fear of judgement and the need to please others. It's about making choices that, despite social norms, speak to your true self.

Always remember that your worth is not measured by how well you fit into the preconceived molds created for you, but by how you break them to reveal your true self. So, embrace who you are, without the masks and without apologies.

Think about the last time you said yes when you wanted to say no. When was the last time you made a choice that was purely for you, not just to meet someone else's expectations? What are the masks you wear that keep you from being your authentic self? These are not just questions -

they're a call to action, a nudge to explore a life beyond fear and cookie-cutter expectations. It is okay to feel scared, it's okay to doubt - but it's not okay to shrink into the shadows when your soul craves light.

Are there aspects of your life where you are performing rather than living? What would living more authentically look like for you?

Keep an "Authenticity Diary" for a month and jot down the moments that you feel like you and the times you feel like the cardboard cutout of yourself.

Make small, daily choices that reflect your true desires, not the social committee in your head. Focus not just on what happened but on how you responded and what you learned.

This will help cultivate a habit of mindful reflection, enhancing your growth.

Commit to one act of authentic living each day such as expressing your opinion, choosing an activity that interests you, or setting boundaries that respect your time and energy.

Here are some words of wisdom for you:

1. **Identify Your True Desires**: Take time to reflect on what truly matters to you, not what you've been told should matter. Spend time getting to know yourself. What are your passions? What makes you feel alive? Dig deep and identify what truly lights your fire.

2. **Practice Saying No and Set Boundaries**: Start small by declining things that don't serve your well-being or happiness. Set those boundaries and say 'no' to anything that doesn't align with your vibe or drags you down.

3. **Cultivate Self-Compassion**: Remember, it is okay to make mistakes. Be kind to yourself during this journey of self-discovery. Self-compassion is the key to living authentically.

4. **Seek Learning in Failure**: Every setback is packed with lessons. After a challenge, take time to reflect on what it taught you. What could you do differently next time?

5. **Cultivate a Support Network**: Build a network of support—friends, family, mentors—who can offer advice, lend an ear, and provide support when the going gets tough. Surround yourself with people who uplift and support your authentic self.

I will wrap this up with this - know that with every step you take toward authenticity, you are moving away from a life of meaningless "shoulds" and toward a life full of meaningful "wants."

With every challenge you face, you are preparing yourself for a future filled with strength, authenticity, and profound fulfillment. You will never experience a more satisfying shift than this one, so embrace the ride and be the oh-so authentic, unapologetic woman you were born to be!

With all my love and wisdom,

Wendy

P.S. And guess what? This transformation sparked something bigger and lit a fire in our soul to encourage other women to unleash their true authentic self and rewrite their life story.

Email: wendyravenjohnson@gmail.com

Facebook: https://www.facebook.com/raven77143/

Instagram: https://www.instagram.com/wendyravenjohnson/

Scarlo Folsom

Being true to yourself is the key

I started working on myself and my business not understanding why I wasn't getting anywhere. I was stuck and struggling. I knew the answers were right there in front of me, but I had no idea what they were or the questions to ask for clarity.

Then I began to hear the words come. The questions started to drip from me. I knew the marketing. I knew the business and old school way of running things. I learned that though it was old school in new school ways doesn't mean I have to change me or the things around me. There are adjustments that need to be made within to create a new process.

After listening and asking questions I was able to see what I was doing and how I was falling off the road. Not feeling my inner self and being true to me. I listened to others and what they felt was the best. I was always doing what they wanted and hushing that voice, that small, little voice to guide and grow.

I discovered I have been doing this my whole life, silencing that little voice, the light being put out or at least attempted to put out. After beginning Consistent Cash and Clients I began to learn this and how to keep my voice in the proper spotlight. Remember that others might mean well, but the truth is that voice needs to be heard. She is smart and has important things to say and share for others to learn and grow.

Through these rounds I have begun to discover my creative and fun side as well as my dreams and how to make them reality. For the longest time I thought I was doomed to do things the way the "traditional" coaches would tell me, it was drab and boring. Then I shared the way I would want to get things done and learned I can do them my style.

Now I am preparing for a new year and a new way of thinking to get things done and grow in my own on the road to absolute success, my style!

Facebook:

https://www.facebook.com/veganrecipeforlife

SCARLO Folsom (@fibro. recovery.specialist) • Instagram photos and videos

YouTube:

https://www.youtube.com/@TheABILITYEquation

Traci Howell

Lead with love

As the youngest of four siblings, I couldn't be happier with my unique position in the family hierarchy. Growing up surrounded by my three older sisters provided me with a front-row seat to a diverse array of personalities, each shaping my understanding of human interaction. In this dynamic environment, I learned early on that communication is not a one-size-fits-all endeavor; rather, it requires adaptability and understanding.

My sisters, with their distinct personalities, served as my initial mentors in navigating the complexities of human connection. Their differences taught me that speaking with others demands a tailored approach. This invaluable lesson in adaptability became a cornerstone of my ability to make people feel comfortable around me.

My observational learning extended beyond the boundaries of my immediate family. Watching my parents care for each other and extend their helping hands to others left an impression that was long lasting on my character. Witnessing their selfless acts instilled in me a profound desire to ensure that everyone's voice was heard, and that people were seen, a principle that would guide me throughout my life.

One vivid memory from my school days embodies my commitment to helping others. A classmate, walking on crutches due to an injured ankle, struggled to pick up his fallen books. Ignoring my teacher's objection, I intervened, asserting that some lessons in empathy were more important than adhering strictly to the curriculum.

This act of defiance resulted in a call to my

parents, but it also reinforced my conviction to stand up for those in need.

Another instance etched in my memory involves a classmate struggling to read aloud, only to face ridicule from others. Unfazed by the laughter, I took it upon myself to help him improve. We spent recesses together, sounding out words beside the school wall. I even provided him with a sack of old books to practice at home. These experiences sowed the seeds of my passion for making a positive impact in people's lives.

As I matured, my inclination to assist others persisted. I advocated for kindness, even if it meant challenging social norms. When confronted with an ultimatum regarding a friendship, I chose compassion, opting to enjoy ice cream with a friend's sister labeled as "resource room challenged" for my companion. Little did I know that these early experiences would shape my professional journey.

Today, I am proud to be an Integrated Content & Operations Consultant, managing my own Boutique Virtual Assistant Agency.

In this role, I continue to observe others, understanding their unique needs, and provide assistance where it's most required. My desire to help people has seamlessly transitioned into a fulfilling career, allowing me to support clients in their businesses, alleviating their burdens and enabling them to focus on their entrepreneurial passions.

My journey from childhood observations to a Boutique Virtual Assistant Agency shares the enduring power of empathy and the profound impact one person can have by choosing kindness over conformity.

Website: www.victoryassistants.com

Linkedin:
https://www.linkedin.com/in/tracihowell-victoryassistants

Facebook:
https://www.facebook.com/VictoryAssistants

Instagram:
https://www.instagram.com/victoryassistants/

Email: victoryassistants@gmail.com

Sophie Bifield

"Pivot"

Learn what and when to pivot. That's it, that's all the wisdom you need in business. Okay, so not the only wisdom, but it's a skill worth mastering if you're going to succeed in business.

I first heard the concept of pivoting early on in my entrepreneurial journey. I can't remember who exactly spoke the words, but I was listening to a motivational speaker or podcast and the guy talking was speaking about how success comes from resilience and resilience comes from the ability to pivot. At the time, I thought he was talking about simply pivoting an idea and changing course if or when your business starts to fail flat. In hindsight, I don't think that's what he meant at all.

About a year into my coaching business, it was failing. I hadn't made the progress (or the money) the internet gurus had promised, and I couldn't understand why. I'd been following my mentor's advice, I'd built all the systems, I'd been doing all the things and pivoting at every turn. Except, instead of pivoting gracefully, I'd been spinning like a drunk ballerina. Pirouetting all over the bar instead of the ballroom and derailing my business right before it had a chance to take center stage.

It wasn't until I found myself staring at the ceiling about to quit one night that it occurred to me that maybe I'd been pivoting the wrong thing. Pivoting was more art than science. It wasn't about changing the direction of your whole business or throwing away the whole strategy. It was more about re-focusing your mind, thoughts, behaviors, habits, patterns and even time, connections, or your environment. Maybe it was more about keeping yourself growing in line with the direction you want to go.

With a new spurt of motivation not to give up that night, I stuck to my business idea, tweaked my strategy, and created an online event in a group I'd been showing up in for a while, closed my laptop and went to bed. The next morning, I woke up to over 300 sign ups to my event. 300 sign ups. I could not believe what I was seeing. I had to triple check to make sure my calendar link wasn't glitching. But nope, it was real. 221 people showed up to the event and from there I launched my first group program, which turned into many more.

What I learned from that experience is that you never know when your idea is going to take center stage, but if you learn to keep re-focusing from distraction and pivot yourself along the way, you'll find yourself in the spotlight before you realize you're entering the theatre.

Sophie Bifield

Connect with Sophie Online at:

https://www.facebook.com/SophieBSocial

Amanda Rose

"Master Your Mindset and You'll Master Your Life"

The key to all the success you've ever chased lies right between your ears – your brain. Our mind is the most powerful tool we have, and yet most people never take the time to understand how to utilize this tool. The problem is, if you don't control your mind, then your mind will control you.

Our lives are mostly habitual; day in and day out, neurobiology has shown that, at least 40%, and up to 95%, of our daily behavior is automatic. What we think, say, and do, are all heavily influenced by habitual automatic responses. This is why people often feel stuck in their lives; when you keep doing what you've always done, you'll keep getting the same results you've always gotten.

If we desire different outcomes, we need to instill new habits. Luckily, we know the brain is malleable, and able to create new neural pathways through repetition, which in turn creates new automatic habits. This is where our work begins.

Your automatic habits happen based on your beliefs, which are stored in your subconscious mind. These beliefs primarily were formed before you were 8 years of age, due to the way the brain develops.

From about age 8 onwards the pre-frontal cortex acts as a filtering system, it's our reasoning center, so we don't readily accept everything we see, hear, or experience, and instead we analyze it. Prior to age 8, the brain acts like a sponge, distilling everything it receives into simple information that becomes the basis of our perception of the world.

Some of those habits are excellent and support us, while others hold us back from achieving the things we consciously desire. A quick assessment of your life can bring awareness to where you have great habits and when you have subpar habits. On a scale of 1 to 10 (1 being terrible and 10 being extraordinary) rate the major areas of your life.

- Relationships
- Wealth
- Career
- Joy
- Health
- Contribution
- Personal Growth

Let's say that you rate your wealth as a 4. We can then look at the belief that's currently in place, by asking these questions:

As a child, around the topic of wealth, what did I:

1. Hear?
2. See?
3. Experience?

Let's say that you regularly heard, "You have to work hard for your money," that you witnessed on TV rich people doing appalling things, and that you regularly experienced school bullies stealing your lunch money.

What you saw, heard, and experienced formed your beliefs around money, which then led to your habits around money. If your beliefs based on those three things were then, "I have to work hard for money, rich people are awful, and it's not safe to have money because someone is just going to take it away," then it becomes obvious that our actions won't support creating wealth, and we will subconsciously sabotage any efforts to create it.

Knowing what those underlying beliefs are, allows us to disprove them, and re-write them. First, pick one of the beliefs, such as, "You have to work hard for your money." Is that an absolute truth in the universe? Is all money hard earned? Quickly we can see this isn't true; if all money was hard earned, there would be a ceiling cap on money we could receive, and yet we often see wealthy people working less, because they have created systems that replace their efforts and allow the money to continue to flow.

Lastly, we re-write the belief into its positive opposite, "you have to work hard for money," becomes, "money comes easily." This new mantra, with repetition, re-writes the belief, and therefore, changes our habits, to create new results. Do this process for all areas of your life and watch as your life changes.

Amanda Rose

CEO of The Infinite Power of You Inc.

https://amanda-rose.mykajabi.com/

Did you Enjoy Reading Words of Wisdom Vol 1?
If so, please Leave a Review on Amazon!

P.S. If you send us a photo of you and the book, we'll feature you on our website!

https://amanda-rose.mykajabi.com/books-by-amanda-rose

Send Photos to:

amanda@theinfinitepowerofyou.com

Printed in Great Britain
by Amazon

48198408R00069